FAMOUS PEOPLE
FAMOUS LIVES

Biographies of famous people to
support the curriculum.

Mahatma
Gandhi

by Emma Fischel
Illustrations by Richard Morgan

W
FRANKLIN WATTS
NEW YORK • LONDON • SYDNEY

First published in 1999 by
Franklin Watts
96 Leonard Street
London
EC2A 4XD

Franklin Watts Australia
14 Mars Road
Lane Cove
NSW 2066

ISBN: 0 7496 3532 0

Dewey Decimal Classification Number: 954.04

10 9 8 7 6 5 4 3 2 1

A CIP catalogue record for this book
is available from the British Library.

Series editor: Sarah Ridley
Historical consultant: Dr A Millard

Printed in Great Britain

Mahatma Gandhi

Over one hundred years ago
a baby boy was born in the city
of Porbandar in India.

Mohandas
Karamaharet
Gandhi
BORN.
October 2nd
1869

That tiny baby would grow up
to be a hero to millions of
Indian people.

When Gandhi was born India was ruled by the British. Britain was very powerful then and ruled over lots of countries.

Indians who wanted good jobs had to learn English.

But many Indians didn't like the British ruling their country.

Gandhi was a nervous and gentle boy. He could only go to sleep with a light on – and even that didn't always work.

He was very shy, too.

No one could have guessed
that he would one day lead the
whole of India to freedom from
the British.

Gandhi's family followed the
Hindu religion, like many
Indian families.

"Kill nothing," said Gandhi's
mother to him. "Pray often
and be as good as you can."

"Live simply," said his father.

"And never eat meat!"

But Gandhi did eat meat in secret a few times. He thought it would make him strong...

...but it just gave him nightmares.

"Now you're thirteen it's time to marry," said Gandhi's father. "We've arranged it all!"

People often married very young in India then. Gandhi didn't even meet his wife, Kasturbai, until just before the wedding.

Soon after that, Gandhi's father fell ill. Gandhi nursed him and hardly left his bedside, day or night. But sadly his father died when Gandhi wasn't with him.

When Gandhi was nineteen he went to London to study law.

He was homesick and missed his wife and baby who were still in India. Even so, he worked hard and tried to fit in.

Three years later he passed all his exams. But dreadful news awaited him back home. His mother had died, too.

Gandhi was offered a job in South Africa. This time his family came with him.

But in South Africa at that time white people treated Indian and African people very badly.

14

On one occasion Gandhi was ordered off a train even though he had a ticket.

"I can leave South Africa now or I can stay and try to change things," said Gandhi. So he stayed… for twenty years.

He wrote about the dreadful things he saw. He forced himself to speak in public.

He refused to obey laws he thought were wrong and the police put him in prison lots of times. But he and his followers never fought back with violence.

In the end he got some of the worst laws changed.

Gandhi was forty-five when he
left South Africa. "Things need
to change in India, too," he said.
Back home people had heard all
about his time in South Africa.
He got a hero's welcome.

Gandhi had made lots of money in South Africa from his work as a lawyer. He had done plenty of thinking about the right way to live his life, too.

He started to work hard for one group of Hindus called the Untouchables. They had to do all the horrible, dirty jobs and other Hindus wouldn't go near them.

Gandhi did, though.

He persuaded the British to treat Indian workers more fairly, too.

Gandhi was now nearly fifty. Britain was fighting in World War I (1914-1918). The Viceroy, the British ruler of India, asked to see him.

"Help me to find soldiers for the war," the Viceroy said. "The people will listen to you."

"You want soldiers; we want to run our own country," said Gandhi. "Perhaps we can help each other."

But instead of rewarding India for its help, the British got tougher after the war.

"Let's fight the British," said some Indians.

"No violence," said Gandhi. "There are better ways to change things."

Gandhi called on Indians to stay at home and pray for freedom instead of going to work. Almost all of them did what he asked.

"Peaceful protest," Gandhi said. "That's the way forward."

But in one city, Amritsar, some Indians beat a British teacher. A British General took revenge.

He ordered his soldiers to open fire on a huge crowd.

The soldiers shot until their bullets
ran out. No one was allowed to
rescue the wounded. Nearly four
hundred people died and over a
thousand were injured.

"No more! The British must get out of India forever," said Gandhi. "We must force them!"

Thousands flocked to join him in the struggle for freedom.

More than thirty thousand people were put in prison for their peaceful protests. The British could hardly cope.

Then it all went wrong.

A big group of Indians set fire
to a police station. Twenty-two
policemen were hacked to death
as they escaped from the
burning building.

"Stop everything," said Gandhi. "Freedom should not be gained through violence."

Gandhi was sent back to prison. It would take another twenty-five years to get rid of the British.

After two years Gandhi was
released. "Now India must unite
and become strong," he said.

He travelled thousands of miles
all over India. "Fight disease!"
he said. "Fight ignorance! But
don't fight each other!"

"You poor, spin cloth!" he said.
"You rich, buy it! Everyone wear
only Indian cloth made by
Indian people!"

Gandhi himself spun 180 metres
of cotton thread every single day.

By now Gandhi was sixty. That year the British put a tax on salt. "Everyone needs to eat salt in a hot country like India," they said. "So the Indians pay more and we get richer."

Gandhi led thousands of people on a long march to the coast to protest. There he picked up a handful of salt.

After that protesters marched on a salt factory. They were beaten as they stood there. Soon, the world knew about this.

Within a year the British removed the tax on salt.

"Who is this leader?" said the British. "An old man dressed like a peasant, yet millions risk prison and even their lives because he tells them to!"

"He goes to prison, he starves himself, but he never fights. How can WE fight such a man?"

"He understands what the people want, what they need," said others. "He speaks in a way that makes them listen. He is the voice of India."

"Some walk for days to hear him speak. Perhaps we should listen to him, too."

Gandhi went to Britain to talk to politicians there. He didn't expect much to come of it, and not much did.

He did meet the King though.

Eight years later, in the middle of World War II (1939-1945), Gandhi made a speech that put him in prison gain.

British quit India!

Kasturbai was imprisoned with him, and died there. They had been married for sixty-two years.

The war ended and the new
British government was ready
to give India independence.

But fierce fighting broke out
between Hindus and Muslims,
the two main religious groups.

"Split India in two," demanded the Muslim leader. "One part for Muslims and one for Hindus."

"A divided India?" said Gandhi. "This is not what I dreamed of."

"It has to be," said the British. And it was.

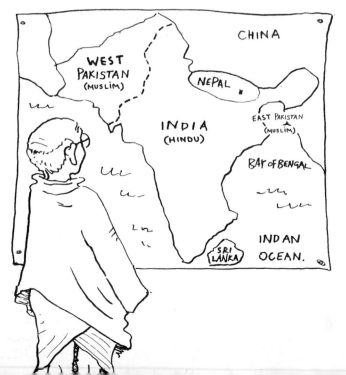

As Hindus fled from Pakistan and Muslims fled from India the fighting went on. Millions died.

Gandhi travelled thousands of miles calming the people down.

But in the end he saw only one solution. "I will not eat until the fighting stops," he said.

"He is near death," said Hindus and Muslims to each other. "We must stop fighting." They were only just in time.

Gandhi was seventy-eight now and very weak.

He knew some Hindus hated him for wanting peace with the Muslims — but he didn't know how much. One day, as he arrived at a prayer meeting, he was shot by a Hindu.

Thousands showed their love for him by attending his funeral.

Further facts

More about Gandhi

Gandhi was given the name Mahatma by a famous Indian poet, Tagore. From then on all the Indian people called him Mahatma. It means Great Soul.

In the second half of his life Gandhi would spin 180 metres of yarn every single day. Even if he had been at meetings until after midnight he would still spin when he got back!

About ashrams

Gandhi lived in ashrams for most of his life. Ashrams were special farms where people lived as simply as

possible and tried to help others.
People in ashrams grew their own
food, spun their own cloth and made
the houses and furniture they needed.

India and the British Empire
The British Empire was made up of
lots of countries, all ruled by Britain.
By the time Gandhi was born, India
had been part of the British Empire
for about a hundred years. Many
British people lived and worked in
India, viewing it as their own country.

Some important dates in Mahatma Gandhi's lifetime

1869 Gandhi is born on October 2 in Porbandar, India.

1883 Gandhi marries Kasturbai.

1888 Gandhi goes to London to study law.

1893 Gandhi goes to South Africa to work and discovers the power of peaceful protest.

1915 Gandhi returns to India in January and starts to campaign for the Untouchables. He also begins the long campaign for self-rule for India.

1919 The massacre at Amritsar strengthens Gandhi's feelings. He urges all Indians to refuse to co-operate with the British.

1924 Gandhi becomes President of the Indian National Congress Party.

1930 Gandhi organises the Salt March.

1931 Gandhi goes to London to meet the King.

1939 World War II breaks out.

1947 India is given independence.

1948 Gandhi is assassinated on 30 January.